INTO THE SNOW

SELECTED POEMS OF

GENNADY

INTO THE SNOW

AYGI

TRANSLATED AND WITH AN INTRODUCTION BY

SARAH VALENTINE

WAVE BOOKS

SEATTLE & NEW YORK

Published by Wave Books

www.wavepoetry.com

Copyright © 2011 The Estate of Gennady Aygi

English translation and introduction
copyright © 2011 by Sarah Valentine

Wave Books titles are distributed to the trade by
Consortium Book Sales and Distribution
Phone: 800-283-3572 / SAN 631-760X

This title is available in limited edition hardcover
directly from the publisher

Library of Congress Cataloging-in-Publication Data
Aigi, Gennadii, 1934–2006
[Poems. English. Selections]
Into the snow : selected poems of Gennady Aygi ;
translated and with an introduction by Sarah Valentine.
p. cm.
ISBN 978-1-933517-53-7 (alk. paper)
I. Valentine, Sarah, 1977– II. Title.
PG3478.I35A28 2011
891.71'44—dc22
2010052077

Designed and composed by Quemadura
Printed in the United States of America

9 8 7 6 5 4 3 2 1

First Edition

FOR CHRIS

CONTENTS

Gennady Aygi (1934–2006) is widely considered to be one of the great avant-garde poets from the former Soviet Union. He wrote and lived during times of extreme terror and suffering in the Soviet Union and because of the repressive censorship, like many writers of his generation Aygi could only publish his work abroad, and even then at great peril to himself and the people who helped him smuggle his work out of the country. That Aygi's situation was so precarious was due in part to his ethnic background, a source of concern in the context of Russian letters and an issue great Russian writers have dealt with for generations.

When we think of Russian twentieth-century poetry, often the first names that come to mind are Pasternak, Mandelstam, Mayakovsky, Akhmatova, Tsvetaeva, Yevtushenko. Perhaps with the exception of Mandelstam, who is widely recognized as Jewish, we generally assume these other writers were ethnically Russian.* But ethnic identity, language, and naming have

* Pasternak, too, was Jewish, and both he and Mandelstam eventually converted to Christianity—perhaps for personal reasons, but also to mitigate the stigma in Russia of being known as a Jewish writer. Tsvetaeva was half-German (on her mother's side) and often switched between the German and Russian languages in her poetry. Mayakovsky was a Ukrainian born in Georgia, while Yevtushenko (born Yevgeny Gangnus) was of Russian, Ukrainian, and Tatar descent. Akhmatova (born Anna Gorenko) was Russian and Ukrainian but took pains to trace her poetic and ethnic lineage back to Genghis Khan. She took the name Akhmatova from her Mongol (Tatar) line to distance herself from a disapproving aristocratic Russian family.

always been sources of controversy in the Russian tradition. Perhaps more than any of these writers, Aygi had to contend with issues of cultural and linguistic otherness.

Aygi's status as an outsider living and writing within an empire had a profound influence on his life and his art. Aygi was Chuvash, a minority ethnic group with its own distinct language and culture living in Chuvashia, a territory located within the western or European part of Russia. Aygi wrote his early poems in Chuvash. In 1953 he moved to Moscow to study at the Literary Institute, where he befriended the aging Boris Pasternak. Although Pasternak became his mentor, urging him to switch from writing in Chuvash to writing in Russian, Aygi insisted on writing in his native language. In 1958 he was expelled from the Institute for his first book of poems, which (because it was written in Chuvash) was condemned by the censors as "hostile poetry."

Throughout his life, Aygi had to contend with the reality that writing in Chuvash would not only mean he would never be read seriously as a poet outside Chuvashia but also expose him to serious political repercussions. Aygi began writing his poems in Russian instead of Chuvash in the late 1950s. Yet in order to balance out the effacement of his native language, he simultaneously changed his last name from Lisin (the Russified surname that had been given to his family) to Aygi, an ancestral Chuvash name—so that readers would always associate his poetry with his native ethnic group. By the early 1960s he was also associating with and writing experimental work inspired by the Russian avant-garde.

In the field of Russian literary scholarship and even among his contemporaries, Aygi's work is controversial. To the American reader who is acquainted with our considerable history of experimental, avant-garde writing, Aygi's poetry may not appear particularly rebellious or provocative in its form or themes. But then (just as today) Russian poetry remained close to its classical roots. Syllabotonic, metered poetry was the norm rather than the exception, not just for official but for dissident poets as well. Poets who write in free verse are often, as Aygi has been, excluded from the canon of Russian poetry.

The subject matter of Aygi's poetry often seems devoid of political content—his writing does not directly address polemics or espouse a particular set of political views—yet writing about what he did in the manner that he did it was and continues to be viewed by many as antagonistic to the hallowed tradition of Russian literature. This has as much to do with his unique biography and background as it does with anything written on the page. For many, this poet's personal history is irreconcilable with the intellectually and aesthetically challenging work he produced.

Aygi drew much of his inspiration from the early-twentieth-century avant-garde, especially Russian Futurists such as Khlebnikov and Kruche-nykh. He was a writer of the Thaw generation, that short window from 1958 to 1962 when Khrushchev officially denounced Stalinism, relaxed media and publishing censorship and opened the Soviet Union to cultural exchange with the rest of the world. Young writers and artists who previously had to smuggle the latest foreign literature and recordings into the country now had free access to the current art and literary movements in Western Europe and the United States. They also had access, for the first time since the beginning of Stalinism, to Russian and other national literature and artwork that had been banned under Socialist Realism. So at the beginning of his career Aygi would have had access to avant-garde poetry from around the world.

After being expelled from the Moscow Literary Institute in 1958, Aygi worked at the Mayakovsky Museum, which is dedicated to the work of Vladimir Mayakovsky and other Russian Futurist and avant-garde artists of his generation. The museum drew an eclectic group of writers, artists, composers, playwrights, and musicians—and the few members of the older avant-garde generation who had survived Stalin's purges, such as Kruche-nykh—and these became Aygi's friends and artistic peer group. Thus, his work engages with avant-garde visual art and music (two of his main influences are the painter Kazimir Malevich and the composer Sofia Gubaidulina) as much as it does with other poetries.

The main challenges of translating Aygi into English stem from his idiosyncratic use of the Russian language and from the nature of the language itself. Russian is an inflected language, which means that rather than using an entire phrase to convey something, grammatical meaning is built into a single word. Aygi's language in particular is very concentrated, and he uses a lot of inflected forms (participles, comparatives, etc.) in his work. Often it takes a long, awkward phrase in English to convey what he says in one or two words. So Aygi's brevity and his sense of the fragmentary, key features of his poetics, are sometimes difficult to maintain.

Another challenge is how to translate small words. Is it *a* man, or *the* man? Did he walk *around*, *through*, *by*, or *across* the field? These may seem like insignificant details, but they are really anchors of meaning in the often abstract and fragmentary world conjured in Aygi's poems. Russian does not use articles, and many of its prepositions can have various translations in English. Because Aygi's poems do not necessarily create a context that provides a single correct interpretation the translator must make that decision on her own.

Aygi is known for his neologisms and his liberties with conventional grammar and syntax. Even Russian speakers often do not know how to interpret the language of his poems. One thing I have learned, though, is that it is usually better to carry that ambiguity over into English rather than trying to force a particular interpretation on the work.

Though Aygi was a committed experimentalist in his relationship to language, canon, and convention, he was deeply connected to a fully humanist understanding of the purpose and value of poetry. His work bears the mark of a deep spirituality in which the poetic process becomes a space for meditation and worship—of our human capacity for creation as much as for otherworldly divinities. Thus the creative force of language is always linked in his work to creation on a cosmic scale.

I think many poets in the United States today struggle with a feeling of irrelevance, of impotence in the face of global-scale crises. Sidelined in a mass-media, technology-driven culture, the American poet seems to have a slim chance of connecting with an audience, and even less of a chance to effect large-scale change through poetry. But elsewhere in the world many poets, like Aygi in the Soviet Union, wrote and continue to write poetry at the risk of losing their lives and livelihoods. For them poetry is an ethical act, an act of humanity, regardless of the cost. Many of Aygi's poems confront the political and social crises of his age, but many others are small poems about the beauty of fields and flowers, the birth of a child. Some consist of only a few lines, a few words, or a single word, or a single letter.

Why bother? What difference could jotting down a few lines about flowers possibly make? The answer, I think, for Aygi was that each word of each poem was part of a grander project, an exploration of the nature of existence, of our place in this universe—whatever that is—of what lies beyond the limits of our knowing, and of how, through a humane art, we can maintain our connection with all of it. Also, and perhaps most importantly, each poem is a celebration of mystery, of the fact that, though we pursue these questions, life in *all* its forms is a mysterious gift. That, if we can find it, there is always enough light—sometimes even on the petal of a flower—to dispel the darkness.

Much of Aygi's poetry is written against darkness, against institutionalized evil, against our tendency to constantly undermine our own humanity and the humanity of our fellows through violence, nationalism, propaganda, and war. His weapon is the exuberance and joy of the poetic act, the ability of language to transform and transfigure a world of inhumanity and suffering into a world of humanity and peace.

SARAH VALENTINE

and you begin to sing — and I am disappearing

slowly into the snow (like before: a figure

darkening in the dusk

somewhere far away) and the broken board appears

there — among the ruins

in the abandoned shack (they sang whispered

then

cried long ago — it seems

from great joy) and in the distance the forest

as if

in a dream

opens — and you are singing

(though — you needn't

for it's already over)

you go on

(though even without us eternity

is already ripening

shimmering

like gold)

you go on

though you're becoming too muffled

to sing

PEOPLE

So many nights
the lines of chairs, frames, bureaus,
I have seen off with movements
of my arms and shoulders
on their regular

and unknown paths.

I didn't notice
how this happens too with people.
I must admit: when I talk to them,
I imagine my finger measuring

the lines of their eyebrows.

And they were everywhere,
so that I did not forget
about life in the form of people,

and there were weeks and years
to say goodbye to them,

and there was the idea of thinking
so that I knew
the patches of light on their pianos
had relatives

in hospitals and prisons.

GIRL IN CHILDHOOD

she goes out
like a bright breath into the field

like board-white buckwheat
cuts through the woods

birds like straw
take the forest sounds on their backs

her pigtails on her back without a plan
as in a dream begin a village
looking over the fire tower's edge

and there in the clearing in the wind
beyond the far heart of the golden rain
a birch plays without a birch
into *u* without *u*

but bright — as if the soul were in a burned-out barn
at night!

and the lake restless as a sleeping
resistance camp: oh just as you would slowly trace a beauty's face
with a white Japanese flower!
across haystacks like white roses
slow and quiet . . . as after excitement
through sparse clearings
in the heart of the place

and those rose-thunder-claps — restless haystacks
to the place of their private conversation
to their brains they open the dragonfly's flight —

brighter than fire down the crucifix-chute!
from present god
to the hill clearing in high darkness

(to the death in blue night
of that faintly shining mind

into his head as if made of roses
dashing themselves down with love)

NOW ALWAYS SNOW

TO N. B.

like snow the Lord is all there is
when all there is is snow
when the soul is all there is

the snows the soul and light
but still just this
that there are those
like death is all there is

to know that they are even here
darkness is also part of light
when the snows come again
Oh-God-Again-The-Snows
as maybe all that is to come

but there is no way to know for sure
as corpses do and do not exist

oh there is the Papier-Mâché-Country
no question what it means to exist
when The People is a verb
that means to not exist

and what does it mean to exist
what's the point of this being
even the Holy Face is just a Mold
that is as if there only is
the country that is Darkness-and-Holy-Face
Epoch-Is-A-Corpse

but there is one thing that exists
when these are suddenly no more
— oh God again the snows! —
they are not just as this one thing is
only Numbness-Country

they are such that they are and are not
and only by virtue of this exist
but there are things that only *are*

a whirlwind as if by a miracle is
in a moment Death-Country is no more
oh God again the snows
the soul the snows and light

oh God again the snows

but should it be that they are not
the snows my friend the snows
the soul and light and snow

oh God again the snows

and snow is all there is

THE LAST RAVINE

(PAUL CELAN)

TO M. BRODA

I climb;

thus

walking

are cathedrals built.

Brotherhood blows us in its cloud:

I (with an unfamiliar word

as if forgotten) and wormwood (that word

pushing near like restless sorrow),

o, once again

wormwood.

Clay,

sister.

And, of meanings, the one that was needless and vital,

here (in these clumps of the slain)

like a name in vain. I smear myself

with it, rising

in very simple light — like fire,

to be marked with the last mark

in place of — the summit; the summit
like an empty face (for all
has been given away): as where painlessness
towers — over wormwood.
(. . .
And
the form
was
not
seen
. . .)
But the cloud:
they became blinder (hollow facelessness),
depths — without movement; light
as from openedness — of stone.
Still climbing
higher.

1

in the invisible glow
of pulverized melancholy
I know uselessness like the poor know their last piece of clothing
and old utensils
and I know that this uselessness
is what the country needs from me
reliable like a secret pact:
muteness as life
indeed for my whole life

2

Muteness is a tribute — but silence is for myself.

3

to grow accustomed to silence
like the beating of one's heart

like life

as if a well-known place there

and in this I am — as Poetry is

and I know

that my work is both hard and for itself alone

like the sleeplessness of the night watchman

at the city graveyard

IN MEMORY OF THE CHUVASH POET VASLEI MITTA

it used to be that summer knew no loss
was softened by the love
of the people of the fields —

as if specially set apart for our clan! —

and life was measured
only by the permanence
of time — that became our own like blood and breath —

only by that permanence —

that demanded on our faces
from simple words
appeared transparent eyelids
and lit up —

from an unseen course of tears

SILENCE

As if
through bloody branches
you clamber toward the light.

And here even dreams are like
a network of tendons.

What can you do? We on earth
play at being people.

But there —
are refuges of clouds
and partitions
of the dreams of God,
and our silence, which we have broken,

because somewhere in the depths
we made it
visible and audible.

And here we speak with voices
and are seen in shades of color,
but no one will hear our true voices,

and, having become purest light
we will not recognize one another.

UNTITLED

brighter than the heart of any single tree

and:

(Quiet places — holding up the highest strength
of song. It takes away hearing there, un-
able to hold back. Places non-thoughts — if you understand
"non.")

The title is stated calmly and softly.

After a long pause, there follows:

A pause, not longer than the first.

The line: "brighter than the heart of any single tree"
is pronounced distinctly, without intonation.

After a long pause:

Another extended pause.

The line: "and" should be pronounced with a noticeable
heightening of the voice.

After a pause twice as long as the previous
one, the prose section is read: slowly,
with as little expressiveness as possible.

AGAIN: IN BREAKS

BETWEEN SLEEP

what watches
always ceases:

and day! and world! . .

unique is
the unending —

is it along its visage that
the soul slides:

like dust! —

and the world of the watcher
does not always open! —

and the shifting dust:

not illuminated! —

is shed

FIELD NEAR FERAPONTOVO

TO I. M.

oh sky-window! . . —

oh into the distant
window
pure and created:

wind — to earth — through crowns of stars:

without noise
without weight:

into the window-clearing! —

into the transparent-cool vessel's
opening — the breath wafted:

into the *window* of man
(over field through field):

into the pure Cup
of mind-perception! . . —

and — completing the together-shining world:

creating its Meaning-Commandment
(resembling Conversation)
with Lightpresence:

wind-illumination! — from sun-window moving away:

into the clear:

limpid-untroubled:

field-window

"SWALLOW": A WAY

OF CONNECTING

TO JOSEPH BRODSKY

there is an M-S *swallow*
for reflection
in the ghostly-glow
of Carbonation-Country:

its fiery sign! —

and by its
seemingly fiery course
they *knit* in basements:

of the Motherland-Glow! —

soon the regular sign
will carve itself out
as a fiery figure:

in your brain — as
in some kind of mouth:

unexpected! —

and it is felt
as the laughter far away:

and broken:

of the past

Do not confront me when I come home:
Open the door, leave the garden.
I have left my needlework on the bench —
I've had stockings that fasten for a long time.

Put the spade in the corner,
Place the pencil stub on the window.
I have read the envelopes in my pocket a hundred times:
That is why in places they are faded, the endings blackened out.

You will not reproach me again:
Shamefully, you forget that I was at home as I ought.
They barely chide a man as they let him go . . .
When I come home do not confront me.

translated from the Chuvash

SILENCE

VERSES FOR SIMULTANEOUS
READING BY TWO VOICES

— ma-a . . . —

.   (but in sleep these very same
eyes
are alive)

— . . . . a-ma.

through God's Pines
shadow-illumination:

a birch-child

PINE ON ROCK

The earth and soil he knew were more raw than that
in which we bury him today.

We are bidding Shalamov farewell.

Literature's body, Poetry's meat, in the "degrees"
of Kolyma's hell, torn from iron with chunks of iron, with
his flesh! — this he achieved.

He was like one dead during life for life. He said —
Absolute: light, squeezed from bone is truer than
if it were from "the soul."

(The living? — they were — "to an extent": they built
plant-"novels" — speaking of the Auschwitz-world; and it was:
a giant fire — in the place that "was"! — with its freezing-to-invis-
ibility ice-pick-"language.")

It means little now that his body is more dead than dirt. (With him
it was like this even before, I knew what happened to the hand
he offered to me twice; read in his work what happened
to his mind.)

We leave here that from which *everything* was squeezed, become the Geometry (we do not see, but know) of Tragedy.

We will return to the city — to the Province of the Living. Where things will be different after today — the space-and-body of Poetry: those living for life do not command Its language.

ROSE OF SILENCE

TO B. SHNEIDERMAN

but the heart

now

or only its absence

into that empty — as if silenced

in anticipation

place of prayer

(pure — presence — in what is pure)

or — the initial pain coming

in spurts (as a child feels

pain)

weak naked-alive

helpless

as a bird

only
one who is hungry
(if he is hard
and free
in thought) —

has lofty-peaceful
purity! . .
(not for anyone else) —

to take
into baptismal
cold —

(harder
than hard:
as the foundation
of pure silence) —

as if in the barren stillness of a field in silence-country *simplicity* had been
achieved —

to absolute-exhaustion

resoundingly consistent to the end:

human — light: as if that last! —

of life for bitter-cold-Russia and a book with no address

AND: ONE YEAR LATER

AFTER THE DEATH OF A FRIEND

TO THOSE WHO KNOW

One a.m.

At this time he slept.

They were sleeping, too.

What lay ahead: waking up, breakfast, lunch.

Errands. Subways and buses. (Motor vehicles, things to take care of.)
Comings and goings. Footsteps.

The manifestation of what was hidden in the soul — ever more manifest
— had begun.

Nonsense in the organs (life-important).

In his pockets — those, and "common" thingies.

Time ticked on. (You can already count the footsteps.)

(A pair: It is clearly visible. To whom? — The city air!)

They breathe.

Spare change, fluids (autonomous-life-republic).

Footsteps — in shoes. (It will be the same with clothing — later.)

Fasteners, belts — like everyone else's (in life all is useful, even after).

Its manifestation — ever faster — in their souls (into the whole, — they explain, — . . . Universe . . . — the brain read so loud-self-assured).

Elevator. The amorphous continuity of moments. (Comprehended as numerals-seconds.)

Footsteps.

(For a long time — quickening-noisily.)

One year. The 26th. One a.m.

They sleep. Nonsense in the organs (both-growth-and-growing). Little things. Lighter. "VT." (Or "Prima.") "Smoke." (Unmistakably it sees a window.)

Dregs-of-the-entire-year. Nonsense — like change in his pockets. Like dust in the creases — nonsense, physiological crumbs.

Something in the air — toward morning.

(SCREAM)

"The life is already leaving . . ." "To D."

It will not be bright.

Day — like a Higher-Blindness. (To them — who must do the same.)

(Easily — like throwing off a robe.)

As after a bath, you massage — by yourself — the last lumps: either your body or a foreign thing.

The easiest (you could sing) world to hide in.

(Clarity. Not weight — from the lumps.)

(Pencil Cretin.) Momentarily — a hole. Such a thing will not slip out of us (we — who have become Fog-Country) at the sight of such things.

But — somehow, look: It is visible! . . — By the light? ("To-D!") — but if only still: By the air! (Vision is — after all — for the Home.)

One year.

(An "anniversary" — for you, too.)

What should poetry do (understood, in this context, in its pan-European sense)?

Not complain about its "condition" or think about its behavior.

In the end it should think about the worthiness of the poetic Word . . . and it is *Johannine* (the definition of the Word of the apostle still holds: "right now," every second).

(The responsibility and essence of our word is in its metaphoric resonance.)

These sayings are not popular or fashionable. There would be nothing left to say if we did not say that.

Not the frequency of "lofty words" but an *orientation* toward the human in his or her connection with nature — with its unchanging *miraculousness*.

To believe in *simplicity* is the foundation.

Not to mimic in order to "suffer," dressing up in "languages" that are alien to poetry (sensationalism, the "news of the day," extremist "causes").

Not to shock the *unfortunate*.

Not to speculate on "despair." (In real despair, art is nearly wordless . . . — for such is the *light* that squeezes through.)

Not only to believe, but to witness itself that man *has not been torn away* from nature.

"The estrangement of man from man." What should be overcome should not be considered "law."

THE SHAMAN AND THE POTATO

FROM "MEMOIRS OF A SHAMAN"

In packages — in the supermarket — piles of potatoes.

And on the posters — in the supermarket — the Shaman.

He is made of stone — outside, in the square, in space, out there (in the Country, around the Country), however, we digress:

here — above the packages (there is something comforting about them) — above the potato pile.

Shaman, even the potato will not remain (not in the store, but in general).

For — Such is Fame: it will not be asked of the Shaman's soul (or rather — of his scent: in a thousand years).

FIVE MATRYOSHKAS

ON THE BIRTH OF MY SON ANDREI

What did you go out into the desert to see?

A reed swayed by the wind?

LUKE 7:7*

1

I am

2

thanksgiving

to the air — the second womb

---

* Luke 7:7 in the Orthodox Bible corresponds with Luke 7:24.

3

with an idea
You surround us
as with silk

4

we are in Time — as if made
of Nature's
veil

5

Surround us
with Yourself

HUNGER — 1947

IN HONOR OF ''SEVEN KREUTZERS''

BY ZSIGMOND MÓRICZ

1

I stood before the bare table on which she lay.

The empty hut — like a box of some universal, empty-indifferent, hollow hours — like even the rustling and whispering was tapped out.

Her mother was there, too (strange, I know, I don't remember).

Wanted it to be even emptier, wanted to knock on all the walls, walking slowly, with a hammer or shoe — just one.

She lay — enduring, immensely, "mortally," in the immortality of silence and rags: dead-emptied-out tatters-flags! — "carefully" — along the edge of the table.

And her legs — fur in tatters: her stockings. As if she rose — on these naked planks — herself, from the garden — from this red-hot haze! — as if — and then she was dead.

Having eaten for a long time, I reckon — it is now 1979 — I can.

2

When a starving person is constantly hungry, for one, two, three years, and so on, he does not know that he wants to eat, he simply — constantly — lives with his "condition" — as if forever! — but one, two, three years pass, and a situation arises in which he *realizes* that he wants to eat. And there, that summer, in those two or three years, it occurred to me in that one, singular incident — glaringly (that's how it was).

I moved forward, legs no longer covering *her* face.

Her face, huge-swollen, that used to be worker-red, horse-red, stayed just as huge-swollen, but glowed . . . fresh, appealing . . . starched. Until, eventually, it looked like a potato, without bruises, without eyes — just freed from its skin, freshly luminous! just barely cooled. (*I will never forget it, as if I saw it yesterday* — yes, those are the exact words.)

And I *became incredibly hungry.*

To draw close, slowly sprinkle it with salt. *This thing*, potatolike, mouth-watering (oh, there will be "poetry," there will). *This* — with salt, and — *eat it, this*, precisely *eat. This.*

KAZIMIR MALEVICH

and the fields rise into the sky

FROM THE LITURGY (VARIATION)

where the labor guard is the only image of the Father
worship is not brought into the circle
and simple planks don't need a holy face

but in the distance — as if the church choir
henceforth shall not know godfather-singers
and is built like a city
that does not know the passages of time

but in those years order was created
by a different, autonomous will —
city — paper — iron — clearing — square:

- simple like fire under ash, consoling Vitebsk

- under the sign of a hint Velimir was given away and taken

- but El he is like a line he in the distance departing

- like a new ending for the Bible: slice — completion — Kharms

- and wrought by others on the planks
the sketch of a white coffin

and — the fields — rise — into the sky
from each star — there is — a course
to every other — star

and he pounds iron
beneath the poor sunset
and the circle is completed: as if from the sky were visible
work so to see it as if from the sky.

SUMMER WITH ANGELS

1. Prologue to "angelic" bagatelles

wind: God lost his cyclamen poem journal

2. The appearance of cyclamens

angels play cards of course angel cards

3. Autumn: fog

birds fall leaves fly south

4. Continuation of the cyclamens

God's geese go to pond

**5. Flowers to the right of the cyclamens
(Christmas star)**

called "mama is getting married"

6. Pleasant vision (or: C-18)

angels are going to school — first grade

7. And to the left — a lone azalea

wind: sniffly God dropped his handkerchief

8. Once again — small flock of cyclamens

angel installation — of Mary's flower

9. The same azalea

and one-eyed God cries in fog

10. Further: C-21 (i.e., twenty-first entry on cyclamens)

angels at racetrack

11. Of course once again about these mag-nif-i-cent

with compasses and rulers angels in heavenly constructors' bureau

12. Unforgettable vision

angels lead Saint Dominic to army

13. And once again returning to them (cyclamens)

confusion among angels in drawing class

14. Ordinary event

angels arrive at "green" congress

15. Once again flowers called "Christmas star"

blushing mama behind loom

16. Simply C-24

angels listen to an angel's new poem

17. Autumn leaf-fall in the garden

and falling days of youth turn up old age

18. Once again they (cyclamens) — like an angelic string ensemble

miniature wings bows wings

19. Here's C-25

angels are the People's assessors

20. C-27 (or: in a certain heavenly workshop)

angel shavings

21. Once again — "Christmas star"

mama under red sun cuts rye

22. Cyclamens' new formations

seconds stopped and put on white hats

23. Simply: cyclamens-34

angels on a plane

24. Cyclamens' latest transformation

seconds put on white gloves and advanced

25. C-37: what *really* happened among the angels

strange: for some reason fluff and feathers fly

26. Once again — unforgettable vision

angel feast

27. Further — C-41

angels say farewell — wave wings

28. And: long epilogue

angel cart moves off and disappears

TALE OF THE

AGING HARLEQUIN

When I used to stroll about,
chess players would follow me in droves
working out their strategies
on my pants.

And when I entered a theater,
all the dolls gawked at Harlequin,
and tried to hide the strings
that jerked their arms and legs.

And when I hid my hands behind my back,
they looked like white flowers
lying on a blue cloak,
and Columbina would sigh after me from the balcony
whenever I walked home.

And when I took off my costume,
Columbina said my hands looked like
burdock blossoms in an empty field.
But the dolls all got married.

And now I sit with Rex the mutt
on an old couch in an empty castle,
drinking coffee, scolding the Siamese cats
and reading the poetry of Yevtushenko.

WINTER BENDER

but to drink — is like sleeping in Summer:

with someone else's
somehow strained face:

above a place non-material
dangerous

and light up in that river
with the invisible fire of darkness

you there my friend
in complete oblivion saying:

"how are we supposed to live? hawking our golden
hides

at the bazaar"

N. KH. AMONG THE PAINTINGS

AT AN EXHIBITION OF M. LARIONOV AND

N. GONCHAROVA AT THE MAYAKOVSKY MUSEUM

once again flashing in the heat
half-rays
half-spirits:

to collect gathering forests . . . . . . —

and in this haze:

the air of the *hundredth* — so they say — *April:*

searches for someone
like delicate cinders! . . —

and — that big-eyed one
who (at one time)
felt the wounds:

reaches out weakly from the empty garden:

to the half-trees
and half-rays —

in the swaying hall

.

DEGREE: OF STABILITY

TO VARLAM SHALAMOV

You are already attended by something like a glow:

and possibly becoming
an icon for everyone:

independent of everyone:

is it the unseen flame of poverty
in the noiseless wind:

its ephemeral face?

or is it the possibility of danger:

in the illuminated faces —

as if
the confessions of the waiting:

are hiding something? —

or — by a hidden flame (as if wearied
by the sight of a patient disease):

everywhere — hidden — striking everyone:

the definitive one
of the Word-Fire:

having long ago embraced
even the places of our premonitions and thoughts? —

is it everywhere as in the silent wind:

no trace no spirit:

engaged with itself?

FIELD: AT THE

HEIGHT OF WINTER

FOR RENÉ CHAR

god-fire! — this clear field

letting everything through (mileposts and breezes and faraway
windmills: still — from this world — in a dream — the horizon: o all
of it — sparks — the perpetual flames of an immortal fire)

alpha-omega — with no worldly traces

immortally shining

god-fire

THIS YEAR'S ROSES

> *In this year's flame I seek*
> *your image.*
> *In the receding Fire.*
> *It is not here — not in this world.*
>
> NOTES ON K. 1972

summer's fire
was the measure of pain — . . . . . . — and how long
did I see you there:

and — worshiped . . . —

this day in the deep glow — only dust:

and — death . . . —

oh it's clear: today's fire is from another
Tragedy of This Place:

and Its cross section — poor and cyclopean
used and discarded:

what's left of hope . . . —

now Its core ignites
the very soul:

even — painless . . . —

but it-used-to-hurt
like your
pain-blossoms:

oh roses! . . —

but *all this*
(I swear) — is you! . . —

be fused — to the final pain! . . — to summer's flame! . . — to your soul in this
Inclement-Land

— Fire-Despair! . .

OUTSKIRTS: WINTER

WITHOUT PEOPLE

it is the glow
of light from light
along the revetment (o empty malleability
of dead resonance! —

o of smooth-free
pure heartlessness
near the heights!) —

even — flowering
(with the juices
of time) —

along the lifeless
gleam
of faux-modern buildings! —

this
glow:
blood —

the empty-colorless — cold! — soul

of cold — so without-breath-of-the-living-emphatically-stern

clear

high

worthy

as it is

READING NORWID

1

I'm in a world of Joy (forgive me, brothers Norwid)
I darken with the shadow of the words: "Yansky Street"
like the D e a t h b r i g a d e in my very soul
I seem to move blackening —

2

and I am happy as a corpse that you're among the living

3

the D e a t h b r i g a d e — the sky above the elevated-Place
now girlish laughter — like your hand

was smeared with poisonous death
a young man sculpts — the day's reflection
along the brow and eyes — like pieces
in R a v i n e – W o r l d of the falsely living
and you are of them: living moving
smearing the others with half-decay

4

when Yearning-to-remain-among-the-dead
when Time-to-leave-the-Province-of-the-living

5

but you are from the T w e n t i e t h P r e l u d e brothers!
through the world a dream
in the last drop of reason
above our heads your a n c h o r
shines — become: last-body-of-the-Day
(even more — as well — my-body!)

I can't recall another! and the exit
will not shine through another Word
having emptied — already without place — a drop

6

o this Unbound-Hurricane with no eye no content — is it into-a-hole-at-
Powązki o God — o the circle long illustrious circle — and haste without
strength o forever without you and even more without this too: without
that piano hurricane and Powązki and the voice — without Fricek's voice
beneath the sky without another sky — there will not be another when
this world without the people of Powązki

7

but there is only One sky — below it like the Senseless-Dead
the Daisy of the Sots-Commonwealth nods:
the same charm: "they-will-enter-they-will-enter-not"

8

and yet — Chopin f o r u s ! — some Johann
by some power
some fire
turn t h o s e s o u n d s — to what? — to make the World-as-Shame
burst into flames (and here some elevated-verb!)
Chopin — f o r u s ! — is it not true — from birth
this (so-called) elevated-Place

9

when Time-to-be-among-the-dead-it's-Time
when Time-to-leave-the-Province-of-the-living

10

and brothers world when joy you brothers
true: they will not separate through light

but shine (and somewhere: "you-must-live")
until "when" others' dead
but only like a corpse a whisper "when"

11

and a discovery, too: they
it t u r n s o u t s q u e a l
when they step on a   c o r n
(is the d i s c o v e r y a t o o l)
....
(for the backwards echo-backwards
as a herald of b e g i n n i n g s
this too will come — materialism)
....
....

12

when Yearn-to-be-among-the-dead-to-Yearn
in space be t i t - f o r - t a t "o Muse"

13

and so advantage we believed
was prison: the more time the better
(was — but left: not about us)
and what's now left for us — Abandoned-cheerfully
by our d e p a r t e d ?
the less prison time the worse

14

gradations of Its meaning
as if you-never-read-it! — and in Dead Silence
I mutter (rather shudder wordlessly)

I repeat them to myself with scraps-of-darkness:
Country-Carbonation — Country-Inclemency
Country-Suffocation and: It's-All-Over-Country

15

when Yearn-to-be-among-the-dead-to-Yearn
when Time-to-leave-the-Province-of-the-living

PAST AND UTOPIAN

1913–1980

(IN CONNECTION WITH KRUCHENYKH)

FOR MARTSIO MARTSADURI

DECEMBER 1980

1

The first and only
fission of the Word.

1913.

Result — the only work:
"dir bul shil."

The fact of destruction.

Glow
of success.

2

Variations of action.

The fission — appearance.

G l e a m   o f   E s s e n c e   —   p o s t - S p e e c h l e s s n e s s .

Ghosts of eidos.

3

The Word is J o h a n n i n e .

The Act — by Example:

Everywhere-point-prayer (as movement-and-stasis),

speech — as a melting:

(By Worldmaking Power —

the All-One),

pause is the fullness of grace,

(old — with no sense of time), —

W o r l d .

REGARDING OUR

LONG-DISTANCE CONVERSATION

TO NIKOLA VUICHIN

1

and he who speaks is not he who has been Word
but he whose step
is like the abiding of an idea — bread in the world
that is simple with such Simplicity
that we speak louder — circling around silence
using up what was added
from the winds of human heaven and the fates
and the gift — like bread — the working Word
it enters into us, gilding
(burning — the natural unity)

2

and, believing, I abide like bread
like food — all giving-opened

for this sky — its mind

so powerful it transforms forces

unmoving stays unchanged

(I was a force among forces I know what I know

and gave myself the greatest gift — freedom

is sometimes only freedom)

SONG FROM THE TIME

OF YOUR FOREFATHERS

VARIATION ON A CHUVASH FOLK SONG

to drink not from the glass, but straight from the pure spring
BÉLA BARTÓK, *Cantata Profana*

I wandered the field there was not
a single haystack

I went down into the village
and there saw
no one

but girls sat
behind small washed windows
and knitted
wide-eyed lace

I looked in the window and saw
them marrying off my sweetheart
arrayed in white
they gave her the cup

— I cried rocking
before your window
and you were silent —

like a candle on the windowsill
of a great church

"I see" I whispered
I whispered "goodbye"
"a people" without kin — I understood
much later
I knew "something happened"

and forgetting everything
I cried with my face
in my hands

LITTLE TATAR SONG

I took a pail and went for water
because we had no water.
I sat next to my pail and cried
because we had no joy.

Back in those days
I was no taller than the pail.

"Mother" I whispered — the meadow hushed,
"Brother" I said — and sleep fell silent.
What I was trying to name was silence:
sun, oak forest, wormwood.

Only to my song,
beyond the aul,
I silently cried — "Sister."

FROM **THIRTY-SIX**

VARIATIONS ON CHUVASH

AND TATAR FOLK SONGS

I

Your figure is a golden wire,
o, your face
from a scarlet flare,
above — the silken air.

II

I had a horse —
you could stretch out on him and sleep!
I could carry water on his croup,
never spilling a drop.

III

Mama sent me on a visit
so that I could rock back and forth
like a sacrificial pot over the fire,
bubbling over before you.

IV

In my father's house
the kindling burns with copper light,
but I still work: my stitching glows like gold!
We don't need the foreign silver light.

V

But her shadow is still there beyond the fence,
tomorrow go — don't stop,
only then will her image
be sealed in your mind for good.

1

the purity of paths
the simplicity of water —

and the sky — as if you dreamed
these heights — not known to anyone
and much — really so much — different
Earth's clean poverty —

in us little speaks:

"while we are in this world
smoke will dance in our huts' chimneys"

2

something dim-white hospital
moved sliding through the field
— God, let this silence heal us —
the road out the window as if beyond gates
fading ever more damp and sad
"this is" as if it whispered "our earthly road"

it is

(perhaps)

the wind

that rocks this too light

(for dying)

heart

RESPONSE TO A FRIEND'S BOOK

TO A. MAKAROV-KROTKOV

here

the figuration of a smile is like an apology

                            asked for in advance

the silence like the nearby presence

of a hidden bird — like when

                            we fall silent and ourselves

(the sound a sign of loss)

when

a "simple" word ("alarm clock" for example)

                            suddenly creates

a forest — otherworldly . . . and the movement

                            of a polikushka-man

along the sad-but-modern Russian Field

X

White — in the meadow — blooms a flower,
— and you are in bloom, the plant in flower —
triumph of the meadow, fullness of the meadow,
ai-iai-yur.

XI

Only in dreams will I go
into our yard,
quiet, my beloved pup,
my tawny songbird.

XII

Scarlet — in the garden — blooms a flower,
— and you are in bloom, the plant in flower —
triumph of the garden, fullness of the garden,
ai-iai-yur.

XIII

The birch's rustling is like a whispered "goodbye,"
and above it
a lonely swift —
like falling scissors.

XIV

The herds stretch toward the watering hole,
soon the dancing will begin in the village —
the whole countryside turned white
from the girls' dresses.

XIX

And in the fog
the green oak
has nothing stronger than a branch
to sing with.

XX

These hands and this head
will remain with those who died in a foreign land —
smoke from the locomotive hits us in the face,
to rob us of memory once and for all.

XXI

And suddenly — peace, as if
I were alone in the world,
and the blizzard out the window, blizzard in the garden,
blizzard in the fields.

XXII

And the day fell silent, like something
meaningful in it had died,
and the fox sleeps in the foothills,
covered by its red tail.

XXIII

Between the Kazakh and Chuvash lands
did you see the post that marks the boundary line?
It is not a post; it is I standing there, petrified
from sadness.

all day the echo of the wind
from
the corner of a nearby field:

visible — delicate — wide! —

but here among peasant
dwellings
it stumbles
ever deeper — as if encountering
"Someone" — of the soul! —

without clarity — without division

LONG AGO

And in a field
the light cried — with wet
and golden spines —

bending over a wall
of unbound rye . . . —

it shone
its cry unchanging . . . —

the World — was at peace.

1

Field and stone.

2

Field — the song sealed up — trembling.

3

Once again — clouds reminding me of something.

4

Dream: Prantl's Field-Hall.

5

Sites of understanding: "He is gone," "They will stay," "Forever."

6

Stone in fog.

7

Bird-cherry — "not for people" (that age — has gone — somewhere).

8

Boulders and shepherd (long ago).

9

Field: the cuckoo's voice — in the distance: the mark of distance — here.

10

Once again — Prantl's Field-Hall.

11

"He," "Will be here," "Any minute."

12

Working and singing in the pine — a woodpecker.

13

Pine.

14

Field — song — as if torn.

15

Hunter and Boulder (like — Book).

16

The sixteenth page: Sun over the horizon.

17

Once again Different Things — among mortal things.

18

And He Sees through the song.

19

Poverty — the engraver.

20

And the sunset glow of dreaming pines.

21

Field: an Orphan's Song.

IN THE MIDDLE OF THE FIELD

and there

goodbye say the roads — the roads say goodbye:

they are startled — finding themselves

in the past (inexpressibly-kindred)

in the future (as if biting

into something "personal" even hostile-secret

life

screaming life)

And a man walks through the field
like a Voice like Breath
amidst the trees, waiting to hear
their Names for the first time.

FIELD — WITHOUT US

the road glimmers, ever closer: like it's singing
and laughing!
light — though full — of mystery
as if shining brighter with its own light
God — endless and sudden! . . — o let
it not falter — let it reach
that abandoned little tree!
swallows sing — shining
like air — over the field ever closer
the wind blows — with something already "homey"
road — like a whisper!
like someone's breath
at the door

ACKNOWLEDGMENTS

I gratefully acknowledge the journals and publications in which many of these translations previously appeared: *diode*, *Circumference*, *Rédaction*, and *Some Kind of Beautiful Signal*. My sincerest thanks and gratitude to Galina Kurobskaya-Aygi for granting us permission to translate and publish Gennady Aygi's work.

I would like to thank my husband Chris for his unconditional love and support and for believing in this project. Matthew Zapruder, Joshua Beckman and Heidi Broadhead of Wave Books: thank you for seeing what I saw and for graciously and generously putting your amazing talents and resources behind the book.

For their generous support, commitment and guidance I also thank: Olga Hasty and Michael Wachtel of Princeton University's Department of Slavic Languages and Literatures, Michael Heim, Francoise Lionnet and Shu-mei Shih of the UCLA Mellon Postdoctoral Program in the Humanities, Peter France, Atner Khuzangai, Gerald Janecek, John Krueger, Ron Gottesman, Reginald Gibbons, Marjorie Perloff, Matthew Shenoda, A. Van Jordan, Ilya Kaminsky, Patty Paine, Yvonne Howard, and CJ Evans and Jeffrey Yang of The Center for the Art of Translation.

For enriching my life with friendship, love, and great senses of humor I thank Tara Anderson, Courtney Carothers, Amy Weis, Alessandra DiMaio, Sonali Pahwa. And last but certainly not least, I thank my parents, Robert and Debra Dunn and my brothers Patrick and Thomas Dunn. None of this would be here without you.